DOWN THE GARDEN PATH

Snippets from the Cottage Gardener

What you forget might just as well have not existed.

Laurie Lee

DOWN THE GARDEN PATH

*Snippets from
the Cottage Gardener*

Sam MacDonald

To my father who made me what I am (for better or worse!),
to all those people who shared long lazy lunches at
The Clocktower, but most of all to my mother and sister
who seem to love me regardless.

CONTENTS

My family home, The Clocktower

INTRODUCTION

aving read Nigel Slater's book, *Eating for England*, I was inspired by his lyrical description of his love affair with British food, warts and all. I wanted to do the same by writing a love letter to the English countryside, and in some part, how it affects my relationship with nature as a gardener in The Big Smoke.

My naturalistic gardening style has been hugely influenced by having spent many happy summers on the North Norfolk coast during my childhood. The wild coastline of wave-battered beaches, calm estuaries (with vast expanses of marsh stretching to the horizon) combined with Norfolk's big skies have influenced many people, from artists to writers to musicians but it had an even more profound effect on me as a young boy.

In fact, I was born in London and have lived here on and off all my life. Despite all its faults I am always drawn back to London, like so many people, and it is not just about money. Yes, there are opportunities here that there aren't in other parts of England, let alone large parts of the world. But I could make a similar income as a gardener working in other parts of the South East because people have bigger gardens and there is less competition. London, however, has a dynamic mix of a huge number of cultures, thousands of years of history (which is surprisingly well-preserved) and a great variety of green spaces sprinkled liberally throughout. You could spend the rest of your life exploring its labyrinth of sights — if you had the time and inclination!

In terms of horticulture, you have the wild expanses of Hampstead Heath and Epping Forest, the woods of Sydenham and Highgate, our well-manicured Royal Parks, the pocket parks in the City of London and of course a large number of allotments, community gardens and small-scale 'patchwork' growers. So despite being a city of close to 10 million people there is plenty to appeal to nature lovers or the green-fingered in our great metropolis.

Although my childhood was idyllic, this was in some ways a bad introduction to the complexities of life because in my teenage years I fell into bad company. This led to my having several periods of drug-induced psychosis in my early 20s. It was in 2007 aged 24 that I finally decided to return to my roots and enrolled in the aptly named course Medicinal Horticulture at Hadlow College. After getting my HND, I began working as a freelance gardener in London with mixed results. Sometimes I have been able to do some of the most creative designs and nurture them to maturity. At other times I have had to do work which resembles the sort of work that council gardeners have to do, such as picking up litter and dog shit. Great fun, obviously!

It is from all these experiences that I draw my inspiration (as well as some of my travels), but perhaps most importantly, from the writings of Christopher Lloyd, Richard Mabey and Beth Chatto. I hope that I can inspire you to enjoy the natural world as they have inspired me!

Sam MacDonald, February 2019

A GARDENER
WITH A LONDON ATTITUDE

Garden Maintenance

*A*s a leading garden designer said, a good garden is 40% down to the designer and 60% to the gardener. The problem is that people are only too happy to pay for an expensive design but then, once the designer drifts off to the next job, have not budgeted for a good gardener to take the garden forward.

It is the same with public projects. Local councils are only too happy to spend money on new projects but at the same time neglect the existing areas. For example, in Dulwich Park in south London they have very successfully planted out a new wildflower meadow in the same style as the Olympic Park but a stone's throw away hundred-year-old rhododendrons have brambles growing through them.

It does seem strange when people talk about the benefits of the new proposed and now mothballed pedestrian garden bridge linking London's South Bank to Blackfriars ('a floating paradise' was how one promotion put it), yet so much could be spent on improving our existing parks. Returning Crystal Palace Park to even a tenth of its former glory would be of great assistance to the local community in terms of providing a much more attractive place for them to spend leisure time and by bringing in visitors from other areas of London and the world.

I think the Dinosaur park, in particular, has scope for massive improvement by using some exotic planting (with big leaved plants from warmer climates such as those used by Christopher Lloyd at Great Dixter). At the moment, the planting does not enhance this great resource left to us by the industrious Victorians. In fact, on June 19th 2018 Time Out reported that The Friends of Crystal Palace Dinosaurs needed volunteers to help with some 'paleo planting' they plan to use (including ferns, ginkgos and cycads) around the existing dinosaurs.

The Cottage Garden

*A*s 'The Cottage Gardener' is the name of my gardening business, I suppose I ought to say something about cottage gardens. Not really an ideal name for a gardening business in London as most gardens are shaded by buildings and trees making them unsuitable as cottage gardens, which need quite a lot of sun. But sometimes a brand, however unrealistic, can get one business because it evokes a positive image in potential clients.

The thing about cottage gardens is the relaxed informality they have. In my opinion, gardens should be places to relax, seek solitude or party; a relaxed and informal garden is the best place to do this. The complete opposite to this is your Chelsea Flower Show garden, which people only enjoy because it's so expensive to build that they revel in the related prestige of sitting in it with a glass of fizz.

A massive problem with cottage gardens or English gardens generally is the amount of water required to keep them going through summer. That is why many have turned to the Dutch Wave movement for a low maintenance solution. This is fine and looks great in September and October but will, in my opinion, never be quite as charming as the cottage garden. Also without being too bitchy, I would say that with the amount of rain in winter in England, leaving the seed heads can look a complete mess.

The Aspirational Plant

*I*n London, it seems that the smartest squares and streets seem to prefer plants to evoke luxury. In Grafton Square (the smartest square in Clapham), St Peter's Square in Hammersmith and many streets in Kensington and Chelsea, it seems that the people who live on these streets want to match the pure white of their townhouses with beautifully pruned and trained purple wisterias. Similarly, the gentle white of a magnolia in the foreground is also effective at creating an atmosphere of exclusivity. Roses can be smart but they can also be common, which is really no good, and something like a honeysuckle is just too charming and rampant to be considered an elite plant.

Non-fruiting cherry trees are also popular and amazingly beautiful when in flower, and unusual types of hybrid clematis can work well as a first rate plant, as can the winter-flowering clematis, *Clematis cirrhosa* var. *balearica*.

Most evergreens (*Buxus sempervirens, Camellia* × *williamsii, Sarcococca* spp. etc.) are welcomed into the richer areas of London, Holland Park being a classic example. The planting is effective but very formulaic so many gardens look similar and therefore lack character. The advantage of this type of garden is that they provide horticultural interest without any work besides the once a month visit from a large gardening company. These companies are famous for having large, smart vans, workers with limited gardening knowledge and a penchant for the extravagant use of machinery, particularly the leaf blower. Please turn that fucking leaf blower off, mate, and get the rake out.

London Garden Schemes

*T*he National Garden Scheme in London is a great day and we're lucky that they have penetrated so many exclusive and elusive gardens. But it's strange that the most exclusive gardens can be so dull. You would think that the squares of Belgravia would have such a large budget that the gardens would be bursting with rare and unusual plants. Alas, the same plants as in your average supermarket car park keep popping up, such as *Aucuba japonica*, *Prunus laurocerasus*, *Choisya ternata* and *Viburnum tinus*. It's such a shame because there is so much variety in the types of shrubs you can grow. But for the sake of low input gardening (in the shade of plane trees), little variety is used.

Nothing could be further from the truth in the allotments also open on these days; they just feel so alive and happy. Surely these are the two greatest qualities to have as a garden because it means they are much loved!

Of course the planting on an allotment is more informal and generally easier to grow such as borage (*Borago officinalis*), calendula (*Calendula officinalis*), hollyhocks (*Alcea rosea*) and nasturtiums (*Tropaeolum majus*). And maybe they might be a bit scruffy, but there is no shortage of character in these gardens despite their humble nature compared with more distinguished colleagues.

Front Gardens

*W*e don't get to see people's back gardens so much. Fortunately, it's not considered bad form to express yourself through your front garden as it is in Muslim countries such as Morocco. I always find it interesting to guess what sort of person lives in a house from the state of their front garden. A popular choice is to put down some weed-suppressing matting and cover the soil with gravel or slate, and plant a small tree such as a standard olive or crab-apple in the centre. As front gardens are often quite small, a strictly formal structure is better because it makes good use of the space and gives the impression of smartness without a huge amount of work. But sometimes formality can suppress the character of the owner of the house, which is a shame. Seemingly, they feel more relaxed with informality in their back gardens!

Anyway, it's one step up from the paved garden or the weed-infested garden. But who doesn't love an informal planting with a mixture of cottage plants such as *Aquilegia* spp., sweet rocket (*Hesperis matronalis* 'Alba'), foxgloves (*Digitalis purpurea*) and alliums (e.g. *Allium christophii*) with some daffs and snowdrops for earlier in the year? Of course, this isn't always possible as the garden may be facing north, in which case a *Fuchsia magellanica*, *Fatsia japonica*, *Hydrangea quercifolia* or *Camellia japonica* would make a useful centrepiece to a small garden.

However, the best front gardens are those that give something for free to the passerby: the sweet smell of *Lonicera* × *purpusii* on a late autumn day or perhaps a few raspberries from overgrown canes.

Garden Envy: When to Plant?

*T*here seems to be a misunderstanding among amateurs about when the right time to plant is. I always seem to get calls around June time asking for a planting but by that stage it must wait until the autumn and there won't be any discernible results until the following spring. You can, of course, plant in spring and early summer but the advantage of autumn is that you can put hardy bulbs in as well as shrubs and herbaceous plants. This allows more spring interest in the next season, because this is when these hardy bulbs usually flower. The problem is that sometimes the winter wet can cause some plants to rot before they have become established. The reverse is the case for spring, when it is drought that usually causes problems.

I once knew an ex-gardener who told me that when he did a planting he would fill in the gaps between plants with extra plants, and then later, when the others had filled out, sneak back and take the extra plants out. I don't know if that was true, but whenever you do a planting the client asks whether the plants are too far apart. A compromise usually has to be reached. Instead of planting shrubs six feet apart often they could be planted four feet apart and if in a sunny spot, bulbs such as tulips, crocus or daffodils could be put in the gaps to fill them out. But this invariably means that in about three years' time, they are going to have to re-jig the border.

Gardening at its Worst

*A*s a professional gardener in London, I've done a fair few jobs that made my stomach turn. But this is the same for all tradesmen. By far the worst has been cutting ivy that has got out of control. It is important to say that professional gardeners who undertake work for which they don't have the equipment are asking for a bill for broken roof slates and possibly even broken joints of their own.

If at all possible, ivy should always be cut in winter (more specifically in January). There are two reasons for this. Firstly, it is illegal to disturb nesting birds and it is quite possible that an overgrown ivy plant will harbour any number of active nests in the spring. Secondly, ivy tends to accumulate dust on its leaves especially in polluted areas, which is very bad if inhaled. It is possible to wet the leaves if it's a relatively small area or use masks, but it is easier to choose a clear day, preceded by wet weather, to ensure that you don't get a lungful of dust. The reason I know this is because I've done it the wrong way (cut it back on a sunny day in April) and regretted it in the pub afterwards as I tried to stop coughing by drinking lots of cider!

The other job that went badly wrong was when I was pruning a *Fremontodendron californicum* and the tiny hairs that are attached to the stem fell into my eyes. I could not see for a good two minutes but was mightily relieved when I managed to get them out, blinking furiously and quietly swearing to myself.

What I have learned from this is that you should not undertake any work that you feel is unsafe. No amount of money is worth damaging your health and most likely the client is not aware of the risks involved in doing the work ill-equipped at the wrong time.

GARDENING
AND THE DARK ARTS

Lady Chatterley's Lover

I've always hoped that I might someday be someone's bit of rough, like Lady Chatterley's gamekeeper friend. Unfortunately, I'm an ex-public schoolboy so perhaps that's why the hope of grabbing hold of some creamy-white thighs with my muddied hands is not really a realistic fantasy!

A few years ago I was a little too honest about this fantasy when, at an unnamed country house with its own picturesque cricket ground, I asked my fellow cricketers if there were any Lady Chatterley types hanging about. Only then to notice that her Ladyship herself was a few feet away with her husband (presumably listening to every word I'd said)! Needless to say teatime was a slightly awkward affair as I desperately tried to avoid making eye contact with her over the cucumber sandwiches.

Lady Chatterley at her gamekeeper's cottage

Mary Jane (*Cannabis sativa*)

*P*erhaps the most recognized plant in the UK because of its well-known medicinal properties! But a stunning plant nevertheless. I often think it's a shame that you need a licence to grow its harmless cousin, the hemp plant, as it would make a better and more beautiful screen than bamboo during the summer although you can only enjoy it for a year as it's an annual. It's amazing how much confusion occurs regarding hemp. For example, it's not allowed to be grown near public roads in case the brainless public get the wrong idea and start picking the buds.

When I was doing my Medicinal Horticulture course at Hadlow College, we learned that various medicinal plants grown hydroponically could be stressed during the flowering period to produce a more active ingredient, by say altering the photo-period (i.e. number of hours of light) by covering the plants under black sheeting for 24 hours before harvest. It does not take a huge jump to realize that this principle can be applied to less legitimate medicinal plants, and indeed there are articles of this sort in *High Times* magazine.

There was also the story of the elderly married couple who bought a plant at a car boot sale and lovingly nurtured it to a size of 10-15ft before they discovered what it was and the police were called in to discreetly dispose of the evidence! There are similar situations with bird feeders when hemp seed falls to the ground and grows into a massive plant (this can happen with other bird-seed such as sunflowers too). Doubtless that is what all the drug-dealers say when they stand in front of the judge. To which the judicial reply would surely be 'Sure. Whatever you say. Now get in with the nonces!'

In case you find this topic a little bit too hippie for your taste, from a mental health point of view I think this drug is deeply destructive. A whole generation of deeply troubled young men and women have emerged as a result of the creation of super-skunk by Dutch hybridizers. In my own case, I deeply regret smoking cannabis in such large quantities or to paraphrase Will Self, strolling across the herbaceous border one too many times!

Champagne

*T*he English wine industry has a bad reputation, which is slowly improving. But apparently the best English wines are the sparkling white wines, a.k.a. English champagne. This is because of the chalk ridge that stretches over northern France, goes through the channel and emerges on the south coast of England. Therefore, in theory the terroir, which makes champagne so unique, is very similar to the south-eastern counties of England. In addition, the average temperature and rainfall are very similar. So why not?

Well, it's all a matter of branding. The French make the best sparkling wine and we know that because everyone drinks Champagne at Christmas – if they can afford it. Otherwise they stay with the Continent and drink Prosecco! Even if English wines were as good, I don't think people would drink them as a luxury item. This is because the best English wines are as expensive as Champagne but without the reputation of being a special treat.

This brings me to a colleague who, every time he visited a certain client of mine, was paranoid that the owners thought he was eyeing up their bottles of Champagne in the garage (which we walked through to access the garden). Anyway, I'd popped out and left him to his own devices when compelled by his inner desires he said to himself aloud, 'I could really do with a glass of Moët right now!' That would not have been a problem had the owner not been in the garage doing some laundry at that very moment!

Red Wine and Cigarettes

I have a special affection for the elderflower (*Sambucus nigra*). The scent of the flowers is evocative of high summer, and I used to play at a cricket ground on Barnes Common in June specifically because the elder trees surrounding it were in full flower. I was always tempted to pick the blooms but was never able to because the terrible rush in the morning of finding my kit (oh shit, did I not wash my jock-strap again!?) whilst eating breakfast and nursing a hangover meant I always forgot to bring some plastic bags to carry my booty in. Also, there was the thought, *What I am going to do with flowers when we celebrate our glorious victory in the pub?* The flowers would have wilted in the car and I would have looked quite strange walking into the Sun Inn in Barnes carrying bags of elderflowers! On the other hand, perhaps it would have sparked some May Day celebrations with young maidens adorned in garlands of flowers dancing round a May Pole! A young(ish) man can dream…

I also had a friend at horticultural college who would pick the berries from an elder that had self-seeded in front of his house and make wine from it. 'The Englishman's grape', he used to call it, and the wine he made out of it was like a decent red and, of course, significantly cheaper.

Funny really, that you are allowed to make your own wine without taxation but not grow your own tobacco. There was an occasion when I was working at a garden centre and a customer asked what a particular plant was to which I replied that they were tobacco plants (*Nicotiana alata* 'Lime Green'). A light lit up in his eyes and he asked if they were the same as the ones we smoked. I replied that they were a cousin but not necessarily good to smoke. Nevertheless, he bought a couple with a glint in his eye. I am sure, since he was a Greek gentleman, that he paid any and all taxes owed to HMRC.

Horticultural Chat

*W*hen I went to Hadlow College they insisted that we get a tetanus shot, a horticultural knife and Felco secateurs. They kindly offered a 10% discount in their shop! As I was buying the knife and secateurs, I met a fellow student who was a little concerned about carrying a horticultural knife around with him in his hometown, Deal. Deal is one of those typical Kentish seaside resorts that has a proud history going back to the Cinque Ports but is now quite deprived. He pointed out, what with the type of people hanging around in Deal town centre, he was not sure if the police would believe him if he said the reason he was carrying a knife was because he was a horticulturalist. In fact, as a horticulturalist or fisherman you have good reason to carry a knife and are protected by the law on this. But I suppose it's rather like a Halal butcher walking around Westminster with a meat cleaver might fall under suspicion if searched.

The other banter I had with this fellow student was about the difference between our two courses. Originally, this college had had just the one course: Commercial Horticulture, which fed the local fruit growing industry with managers. However, interest in this compared with other career paths had declined to such an extent due to the poor pay and long hours that the college set up another course called Medicinal Horticulture. My fellow student did not take this course entirely seriously and felt that it did not deal with the realities of commercial horticulture. Doubtless, he imagined me skipping out to the garden by the light of the full moon and picking some lavender for another herbal infusion. He was partly right. Although the Medicinal Horticulture course was fuller than Commercial Horticulture (he was the only student that completed that course I believe), it *was* filled with people who had no interest in 'going into the industry', as our tutor used to say rather overenthusiastically.

PLANTS I'VE KNOWN
AND LOVED

Snowdrops (*Galanthus spp.*)

*T*he snowdrop ranks highly, in my humble opinion, as a flower that cheers you up. Probably because they come at such an improbable time of year (late January/early February), they are well thought of. Like a clump of primroses, there is a sort of innocence and spring freshness about them as they hang like dainty little bells just above the partially-frozen ground.

Galanthophilia takes this a bit too far though. I can't get that excited about all the different types of snowdrops. Certainly not to the extent that I would pay £20 for a single bulb when they are a plentiful semi-wild plant. For example, at Walsingham Abbey in Norfolk (between Wells and Fakenham) they have naturalized through acres of undulating woodland so it can look like a sea of white and tiny bells swaying gently in the breeze. This is because of the humus rich, constantly damp (but not waterlogged) soil, which is slightly alkaline. They have spread so much because the conditions are presumably so similar to their native habitat of south-eastern Europe and Asia Minor. It has taken them hundreds of years to do so because they were probably originally planted as a symbol of Candlemas, which was a festival to commemorate the purification of the Virgin Mary after childbirth. It was celebrated on the 2nd of February, when religious symbolism was at its height, in Medieval Times.

Wild Strawberries (*Fragaria vesca*)

*N*ot only is the fruit of the wild strawberry extremely delicious, delicate and exclusive but also it makes an easy and versatile garden plant. This is because it has pretty *Rosaceae* shaped flowers in spring and attractive distinctive foliage throughout the year and is tolerant of a wild variety of soils and situations.

Similarly, its pure white flowers with their yellow centres combine well with the Snake's-head fritillary (*Fritillaria meleagris*) in April to create an impressive springtime drift in herbaceous borders.

As if that's not enough, being able to rummage around in the undergrowth in mid-summer and emerge with some wild strawberries from your own garden can seem very sophisticated. Indeed, one of my previous clients, who was a bit of snob, found it very satisfying to do this for his guests at barbeques. Often found growing wild in abandoned gardens and railway sidings and with a preference for chalky soil, wild strawberry plants are something I always take great pleasure in finding in the wild.

There is one slight problem with picking the fruit in that it must be completely ripe to taste delicious and it's hard to get it at that precise moment. Still, it's far superior to its bigger brother, that bland brute of a strawberry grown in polytunnels!

I would like to eat my wild strawberries in the same way as Gerald Durrell's pet tortoise, Achilles, described in his book, *My Family and Other Animals*.

'[Achilles] would become positively hysterical at the sight of them, lumbering to and fro, craning his head to see if you would give him any, gazing pleadingly with his boot button eyes. If you gave him a big one ... he would grab the fruit and ... stumble off at top speed until he reached a safe and secluded spot amongst the flower beds where he would ... eat it at his leisure.'

Fatsia Japonica

*T*o me, one of the most effective plants to use in a London garden is *Fatsia japonica*. It is so undemanding of sun, water or feeding. It is very useful as a part of an exotic garden, completely hardy in a London garden and could be used as a centrepiece for a front garden particularly on a north-facing wall.

Like its cousin, the most feted (and in turn hated) ivy (*Hedera helix*), pruning *Fatsia japonica* is relatively straightforward, as all but the most brutal cutbacks will not stop it from regenerating. Perhaps the link between these two is most apparent when you see the similarity in their flowers, which appear in late autumn and persist into early winter.

The best cultivar in my opinion is 'Variegata' but a newer cultivar, 'Spider's Web', is quite nice with a sort of marbling variegation on it. Also, there is a cross between *Fatsia japonica* and ivy called *Fatshedera × lizei,* which can be used to make an interesting change in a shaded garden – although it does flop over a little. This doesn't allow it to show off the shape of its beautiful leaves to the same extent as its parents'. Which is a shame because I think its shape is the best possible compromise between the very compact ivy leaf and the slightly oversized *Fatsia japonica* leaf.

Self-Seeders

I like a naturalistic style of gardening so whatever self-seeds in the garden can provide valuable interest at no extra cost (I have Scottish ancestry so meanness is something that comes naturally to me). Perhaps the best self-seeder in terms of getting a great plant for nothing is the foxglove (*Digitalis purpurea*). It will sow itself in the most unlikely of spots. For example, I remember Beth Chatto, the famous plantswoman, once commenting on how surprised she was to see foxgloves in film-maker Derek Jarman's garden, in the wind-swept desert of Dungeness, when its natural habitat is woodland clearings.

My next favourite self-seeder is the opium poppy (*Papaver somniferum*) and there are some beautiful shades of it, which put to shame the very ordinary knicker-pink one. I particularly remember a patch on some waste ground near the RSPCB beach at Holme in Norfolk, where some stunningly beautiful red and black coloured ones had seemingly self-sown under an information sign there. I kept meaning to go back and collect some seed but always forgot. Poppies are interesting because their seed must not be covered with soil or they will not germinate. This is why, when fields are ploughed, corn poppies (*Papaver rhoeas*) seem to germinate like weeds because the seed is churned to the surface by the plough. This irritates farmers hugely but provides an interesting contrast in a field of wheat for cyclists and walkers. In fact, because of this, it is something of a symbol of the stretch of North West Norfolk, which I am so fond of.

Herb Robert (*Geranium robertianum*), Herb Bennet (*Geum urbanum*), Lesser Celandine (*Ficaria verna*) and Alkanet (*Pentaglottis sempervirens*) all self-sow prolifically in my London gardens but despite being very pretty are all pernicious weeds that need a firm hand.

The forget-me-not (*Myosotis* spp.) needs a special mention here because it always seems to pop up in people's gardens and makes a significant contribution in spring to any combination in cottage gardens when mixed with tulips and/or wallflowers. Managing the process is easy as you can pull 99% of the plants up when they are over and still find enough seedlings for next year because the top may still be flowering when the bottom flowers have already turned to seed. Nice little trick that!

In terms of plants you need to introduce to your garden but will then self-sow: Californian poppies (*Eschscholzia californica*) are fantastic in gravel, *Nigella damascena* is a great filler in part shade and the Poached Egg plant (*Limnanthes douglasii*) is a useful weed-suppressing groundcover in dappled shade to full sun under shrubs and trees. *Calendula officinalis* can be a show-stopper when planted in drifts (such as at Eden Community Garden in Clapham, London) and Honeywort (*Cerinthe major 'Purpurascens'*) is a delicate addition that gently self-sows. Finally, for a shaded spot, Honesty (*Lunaria annua*) is almost quite invasive in its self-seeding when you manage to find a spot that it likes.

Lungwort (*Pulmonaria officinalis*)

*S*uch a hard-worker this plant and very promiscuous as well (it self-seeds everywhere in my garden). Certainly the bees love it as there is very little in flower so early in the year. Its spear-shaped leaves with white speckles continue its contribution to the garden later in the year.

Its shape and speckling was considered significant in the Middle Ages and for several centuries afterwards because it was based on the highly dubious doctrine of signatures. This meant that doctors believed that since pulmonaria's leaves looked like the lungs, they would be good at treating ailments of them. Hence the name lungwort!

It prefers shade but will tolerate sun if the soil is moist. There is a dazzling array of cultivars from 'Lewis Palmer' (pink turning to blue) to 'Blue Ensign' (silvery leaves and azure blue flowers) to 'Sissinghurst White'. The last time I checked, it was £4.25 in the garden centre for a named cultivar of pulmonaria and so I make a habit of giving my seedlings as presents to garden-minded friends.

Herb Bennet (*Geum urbanum*)

*T*his plant is a seriously invasive weed. Still, I can't completely weed it out because its flowers look so dainty and it seed-heads so attractive. I did notice last June in midsummer that all the herb bennet were seemingly flowering together and then the following week they all had seed-heads, which made me wonder whether they danced together all through the night on midsummer's eve...

When I mentioned my liking for this plant to another gardener he also said he had a soft spot for it, because he had apparently watched a dormouse repeatedly bend the seed-heads over to collect the seeds for snacking on.

Salvias

*S*alvia microphylla* 'Hot Lips' is one of the most popular salvias used in cottage gardens because it can flower for extremely long periods. It can bloom from May until November if the weather is favourable. This is an impressive effort compared to some plants. Cherry trees, daffodils and peonies, which flower for about 3 weeks, are praised to high heaven and then forgotten about for the rest of the year. *Salvia microphylla 'Hot Lips'* is quite garish early in the season but mellows through the season as its flowers turn from pure red to pure white. It is not a plant I use any more, but its relation, the straight *Salvia microphylla,* seems a more refined plant in a sheltered, warmish garden. Such is the lack of real cold weather in the winter these days that it is considered quite safe to grow it over winter in London and indeed, places further north have had similar success. For example, it grows quite happily along the coast in Hunstanton, Norfolk and also in the Yorkshire Dales (although it must be quite likely you would lose it there over an average winter).

Salvia nemorosa 'Caradonna' is also an effective and popular plant whose purple-blue flowers can be used as a hedge replacement for lavender if, for example, the soil has proved too heavy for the lavender. It also mixes well into herbaceous plantings and is popular with bees — always a bonus.

Salvia 'Amistad', like most salvias, is a show-stopper in the gentle sunlight of October and very undemanding, although I have always found *Salvia patens*, which is often offered in the garden centre in late summer as a filler, a little disappointing and unreliable.

Perhaps my favourite salvia is *Salvia sclarea* var. *turkestanica*. It's a biennial or sometimes a short-lived perennial with handsome pink-tinged white spikes of flowers growing out of it. It can reach quite a size, up to 4 feet, and has a peculiar scent sometimes unkindly likened to BO! In case you were wondering; the reason I like it is that it is very easy to grow, you can pot up the numerous seedlings that it produces and it is a very architectural plant for a herbaceous border which can often lack contrast in leaf shape and height.

Far-flung and warmer climates offer many other plants like the salvia, which flower for long periods of time and thus earn their keep in the garden, such as the varying array of fuchsias (e.g *Fuchsia magellanica)* and hebes (e.g *Hebe salicifolia*) to name two that I use quite a lot in sheltered London gardens. This is because the life cycle of these plants is limited by temperature instead of daylight so they will keep flowering if the temperature is warm. In some of the milder winters we had in the early 2010s in London, it was possible to see hebes, salvias and fuchsias still in flower in December, which does in part explain their usefulness.

CHILDHOOD
AND THE GARDEN

Weeping Willows

*W*hen willows (*Salix* spp.) come up in conversation the first thing I think is *The Wind in the Willows*. Still with one foot in my childhood, I remember fondly the innocent wonder with which I enjoyed the adventures of Ratty, Mole and Badger in the wild wood or when they were 'messing about in boats'.

Next, I think of cricket bats because the English white willow (*Salix alba* var. *caerulea*) is still the best source of this. Roger Deakin, in his book *Wildwood: A Journey Through Trees*, summed it beautifully (sincerest apologies to my Aussie friends on this!) when he said:

> You can make a decent bat only from the wood of cricket bat willow [*Salix alba* var. *caerulea*], and the trees will grow really well only in England, preferably in Essex or Suffolk. People manage to grow them with moderate success in Kashmir and Australia ... but the poor willows aren't really happy. As a result Kashmir willow is too heavy ... and the Australian willow is ... strangely coloured, because it must be ... artificially watered ... It remains a source of deep frustration to Australian cricketers that to obtain a top quality bat, they must still import the willow from England.

Despite my love of cricket there is something very sad about the thought of cutting down a majestic willow for the sake of a few cricket bats! This is because the weeping willow is the most beautiful tree – apart from Western Hemlock (*Tsuga heterophylla*) perhaps – when it's being blown around by the wind. Perhaps, the willow is the goddess of the waterways, with its long mop of leaves not unlike the flowing hair of a woman, charged with the task of safeguarding the rivers and streams of England.

The Wild Cherry Tree

*C*herry trees are very special landmarks in the countryside or people's gardens, and the taste of a really good cherry is evocative of high summer. We had a wild cherry tree in our garden and I used to lick my lips all summer at the thought of my mum's wild cherry ice cream. Wild cherries are very tart when raw but when cooked with sugar are utterly delicious.

It was a great sadness to me as a little boy when my parents said that they were going to cut the cherry tree down because it was too close to the house. I still feel sad about it however practical the reality of the situation was.

I did plant another cherry recently but it has not been nearly as successful; the birds always get the fruit. So the only time I get to eat really delicious cherries is when I go to Brogdale's Cherry Fair in Kent, and oh my god, the cherries are fantastic. So many different types and colours, full of flavour because no thought is given to how they travel or are stored (like so many tasteless supermarket cherries). A personal favourite is called 'Turkish Black', which has very dark and quite small fruits, but a richness of flavour that's just divine! Combine it with a trip to Broadstairs (for fish and chips) and you have a fantastic day out.

A Ghost Story for Christmas

*M*y sister introduced me to M. R. James (whose ghost stories were turned into a series of short films as Christmas specials) in the 70s and in the early 21st century . His stories struck a chord with me because many of the films are set on the North Norfolk coast, which I know intimately. His haunting description of solitude, particularly when walking on an empty beach, is familiar to East Anglians in particular but not exclusively.

Here is my own attempt at a horticultural ghost story for Christmas.

De Wynter was a very queer man. He lived in the ruins of what had been the great Harpingdon Hall, a rambling house with turrets and chimneys originating from the 16th century. He had squandered his inheritance on booze and was frequently seen glugging a bottle of wine in the overgrown gardens of the Hall. There was only one employee left called Williams and he slept in the woodshed because he had nowhere else to go.

One day, De Wynter was stumbling about the gardens when he tripped and fell into the remains of what had been a very fine yew walk. Once he had composed himself he saw Williams coming towards him and said, 'Cut these bloody trees down you oaf! Can't you see they're getting in my way!'

Williams replied, 'But sir, you can't cut these trees down. It's bad luck. We don't want evil spirits haunting us!'

'That's all rot! Fetch me an axe!'

'No sir, I will not. They say the Gypsies lay offerings under the ancient yew at the end there to appease evil spirits and I don't intend to offend the spirits myself.'

'Damn your eyes, man. If I was paying you anything I'd sack you.'

He staggered to the end and looked quizzically at the posies the Gypsies had left of dog rose, old man's beard and wild geranium. He kicked childishly at the pile, grinding the posies into dirt, and stomped back to the hall. Williams, having seen all this, looked worried but said nothing.

That night a great wind blew from the west and the trees shook loudly and vociferously in the park. It was almost as though they were singing some tragic song together.

De Wynter suddenly awoke from his drunken slumber and heard the singing. He looked out the window and could see many lighted candles held by someone or something moving around at the bottom of the driveway. It scared De Wynter to no end and he rang the bell. Williams eventually arrived and said, 'It's the Gypsies, sir. They are unhappy about what you have done. You must make an offering to the ancient yew or we shall be cursed for all eternity!'

De Wynter took him more seriously this time. He said, 'Alright man. Tomorrow I will do so but get these flaming gippos back to Gipsy Green or I'll set the dogs on them.'

'They won't go sir,' Williams replied. 'I have already tried.'

And so all night the wind howled and the sound of singing and lights haunted De Wynter's soul.

In the morning Williams brought him his breakfast but De Wynter seemed struck dumb and could not speak a single word. And so it was that the Gypsies returned for three more nights and each night De Wynter grew more and more haunted until finally on the fourth day Williams arrived with his master's breakfast to find him gone without trace.

And so it is said that De Wynter's soul was taken by the tree and that no one should tread in the gardens of the hall at night in case they should meet De Wynter's evil spirit.

Peter Rabbit
and Mr McGregor's Garden

*W*hen we were growing up I loved the Beatrix Potter books but particularly the story of Peter Rabbit. Near us was an old walled garden where a grumpy old man (much like Mr McGregor in the book) used to grow flowers, fruit and vegetables. We were scared that he'd chase us out of the garden and we'd have to go to bed early with a cup of chamomile tea.

I was reminded of this when one of my childhood friends arrived with her two daughters at my childhood home and my mum gave them the DVD of Peter Rabbit. It didn't seem that long ago that we were the children! It's with a certain sadness tinged with joy that the wheel of life has moved on and that all I have left of those days is the memories I share with friends and family about that time. I hope it means that those memories are not gone but are passed on to the next generation.

Unfortunately, time forgets us all. You only have to look at the decaying splendour of the Magnificent Seven cemeteries in London to see that no one remembers our Victorian predecessors intimately however extravagantly they tried to etch their names into history.

THE FIVE SENSES

Sight

A divisive subject to say the least. I do not pretend to have the impeccable good taste of interior designer Nicky Haslam, for example, who would probably walk through the houses and gardens of many suburban streets repeating the phrase 'How very common!'

What I do know is that many of the plants available in late summer are from the prairies of North America and as many of these plants are from the daisy family (whose flowers are often yellow) there is little to be done but to use them carefully. Of course in spring and early summer, it is much easier to use an understated pastel scheme with pinks and whites and blues. A gardener can easily obtain perennial geraniums, hostas and roses to match this colour scheme. What these plants will look like in late summer is another matter but perhaps the owners will be in the French Riviera by then so it won't be a problem!

However, there are some good alternatives without yellow flowers that I would highly recommend to keep the garden looking well-furnished into late summer. First, there is *Verbena bonariensis*, the slinky supermodel (as one magazine writer described it!) that was first used in pricey garden design projects but then became so widely available that now every suburban garden has it. It is rather like the *Choisya ternata* in this respect: so good at its job that it is overused.

Another plant I think highly of is the marshmallow (*Althaea officinalis*). No less than a British native (albeit an endangered one) which flowers in late summer because it lives, surprisingly, on marshes, mainly in the east of England, which warm up slowly. Easy to put at the front of the border as long as you know where it is. It may need staking as rich soil makes it flop over.

Finally, there is the echinacea, which is as well-known as the *Verbena bonariensis* thanks to the Dutch Wave movement. Usually pink or white, although if you want a yellow one I believe there is one called 'Mac'n'Cheese'! When I talk about echinacea I mean *Echinacea purpurea,* which can be a little tricky. It does not tolerate drought but will rot if given an excess of water. In its natural habitat it grows on the edges of woods in North America but full sun in the UK is fine because our sun is less intense.

Sound

*O*ur sense of hearing is perhaps the most underrated sense in the garden but there can be something truly magic about hearing an ash rattle in an autumnal wind or a gentle breeze causing ornamental grasses to rustle in the same way we might sigh.

There is also the gentle buzz of bees collecting nectar, from say crocuses, in the bright sunlight of early spring or the sound of water gently gurgling in a small stream.

To say nothing of the blackbird in April or the solitary robin singing its heart out at Christmastime when there is a dusting of frost on the ground.

I also enjoy the sounds of some human or animal activity, such as the gentle hum of the mower or the singing or music making of a fruit picker, Gypsy or wanderer, such as the rose beetle man in Gerald Durrell's *My Family and Other Animals,* which documented his adventures in Corfu:

> He had a fairy tale air about him that was 'impossible to resist' ... I first saw him on a high, lonely road leading to one of the remote mountain villages [of Corfu]. I could hear him long before I could see him, for he was playing a rippling tune on a shepherd's pipe ... and above his head, circling drowsily round and round, I could see the dim specks that were the rose beetles.

You'd be lucky to hear that in England these days such has our economy developed and population grown! However, there is still the bleating of sheep that you get in Yorkshire Dales, which seems to fit the atmosphere of that deliciously green landscape.

Taste

I think the most important thing to remember about good eating and its relationship to gardening is the importance of eating locally and seasonally. Whenever you eat any type of food whether it be scrumped apples in September, the first sorrel of the season (served as a dressed salad with a creamy omelette in March) or indeed the first new potatoes in June dripping with butter and parsley, the flavour will almost always be fantastic because you are eating seasonally and locally.

As fruit and vegetables are increasingly treated like commodities by supermarkets, their flavour is severely affected. This is because they need to be transported huge distances and stored for quite long periods of time before being sold which affects the ratio of sugar to starch in them and requires the use of preservatives that can alter the flavour as well.

People who are not interested in gardening argue that with vegetables so affordable, given most people's incomes in London, it makes little sense economically to grow them. But you cannot buy taste in the supermarket and that is why, in part, people are drawn to allotments and community gardens. Also, it is nice to know the story behind those knobbly carrots you are serving at your dinner party, and yes, they do taste all the better for it!

Smell

*T*he scents that are most often talked about in the garden are of flowering plants during the heady days of summer: the scent of jasmine on a summer's day or perhaps that of honeysuckle in the evening. I have to say that although I value the mixture of scents you get from these and other summer flowering plants, it's the different and wide variety of scents from winter flowering plants that turn my head if only because they are so unexpected. For example, *Viburnum* × *bodnantense* 'Dawn' with its roast beef smell or the delicately spiced scent of a witch-hazel (*Hamamelis* spp.).

Other scents I relish in the garden are those of the season, such as decomposing leaves in autumn or the smell of wood-smoke in winter or alternatively the smell of a *Choisya ternata* when it is being pruned in late spring/early summer. I'm not sure I share the same enthusiasm for fox shit or comfrey tea as the anti-hero of Patrick Süskind's brilliant book *Perfume,* who does not distinguish between good and bad smells. But there are far more good smells in the garden than we acknowledge beyond the well-known and slightly cloying rose's scent.

Touch

*T*he plants I think of most often, in regard to touch, are grasses (e.g *Stipa tenuissima*) and those soft-leaved plants usually associated with the Mediterranean, e.g. lamb's ears (*Stachys byzantina*). Brushing against that type of plant can add an entirely different dimension to a garden because rather like very soft hair it evokes the gentle beauty of youth.

I also get the same feeling from lying in slightly long grass whilst twirling daisies and looking at the clouds. I don't think there is any blanket that feels quite as comfortingly soft as a field of grass. Similar to this is the feel of a gently flowing stream, as you dip your hand in it from a boat while you drift down on the current. With the soothing sound of the river, the fresh feeling of the water and the softness of the weeds it can remind one of the June freshness with which Evelyn Waugh described Sebastian Flyte and Charles Rider in *Brideshead Revisited* drifting down the Thames on a punt.

Similarly, driving through the winding lanes of the English countryside in May with the verges frothy with cow parsley and the rush of the wind in your face is an equally exhilarating experience. It allows you to almost become one with the natural world as you purr through it in a classic car. Or at least that's what I imagine driving an AC Cobra in Norfolk would be like having jealously watched others do it!

THE FOUR SEASONS

Winter

I have tried very hard to like winter but failed miserably. However, on a cold crisp sunny day following a long walk in the countryside and a hearty steak and ale pie in a traditional pub it can seem quite lovely. But since there is so much cold, wet and dark operations in the garden can become more theoretical. Staring at the garden through the window, imagining beds full of colour and life instead of lifeless soil, or flicking through seed catalogues by the fire are two such activities that barely fill the hours of void.

In fact, most parts of England are very lucky to have quite a few days which are mild enough for you to get into the garden and get ahead with the tasks that need doing by the beginning of spring, like spreading manure, removing fallen leaves or removing dead material from perennials to make way for the new growth that should begin to peek through. It is the only time a professional gardener can, at his leisure, do the necessary tasks properly, knowing that the deadline is some way off.

Despite this, I agree completely with Rosemary Verey when she said, 'I could do without January'.

Spring

*T*he seasons are often compared to the progression of the human life. Spring is childhood, summer youth, autumn middle age and winter old age. Of course it's natural for our lives to mirror the cycle of the natural world however much we try to detach ourselves from it with technology.

The most startling comparison between the natural world and the way human life develops was made by nature writer, Richard Mabey, when he compared the scent of Moschatel, a very early spring flower, to the smell of his first girlfriend. He summed it up hilariously by saying that the mind boggles at the bio-synthetic pathways that link the scent of a pubescent girl to a spring flower. When I mentioned this to my sister, her reaction was typical of the age we live in; she said he was probably a kiddy fiddler! (He definitely is not he's a happily married man, just to clarify that!)

Summer

*I*t's a happy time if not the happiest. It does not matter whether you are a gardener or not. It is hard not to feel romantically involved with a season that sweeps you along with its joyful exuberance whilst making so little effort.

Most of all it makes me think of my summer holidays in Norfolk as a child. There would be the hum of the TV, as my father cursed another thrashing by Australia in the cricket (a common occurrence in the 90s). The kitchen would be a hive of activity as various pots bubbled away as my mum made jam, cake and stew all at the same time. In the background the doves, in the Austrian pine nearby, cooed pleasantly and the sun never seemed to stop shining.

Much like Gerard Durrell in *My Family and Other Animals,* I would bolt down my breakfast and head out into the countryside. I would cycle endlessly up dusty tracks through bright green hedgerows. I took great pleasure in the picture postcard villages littered by exquisite medieval churches. I also loved the rush of going as fast as I could down the hills as swallows and breath-taking views swept by. I still wish I could go back to that time even for a day. Of course the only way I can repeat my childhood is by having children of my own. That does not seem very likely at this stage, which is sad in some respects but liberating in others.

Autumn

*S*eptember is my favourite month mainly because you seem to be getting an extra month for free. When the calendar turns over to the 1st of September, even when my schooldays were long behind me, I still thought, *Well, that's the summer gone.* But so often there can be many days to enjoy before the rains of October. Especially in the summers of the early 2010s, it seemed the only time you could rely on some sunshine in the southeast was in September. Indeed, the rest of the country probably didn't get a summer at all!

But it's also partly the light. It's so soft at this time of year and is even more accentuated by the exotics that are reaching their peak at this time like *Helenium* spp. (e.g *Helenium* 'Sahin's Early Flowerer'), *Fuchsia* spp. (e.g. 'Lady Bacon'), *Salvia* spp. (e.g *Salvia* 'Amistad'), *Dahlia* spp. (e.g. 'Bishop of Llandaff'), to name but a few.

Also, September is harvest time with many vegetables coming from the allotment, particularly runner beans, potatoes, tomatoes and courgettes. My James Grieve apple fruits and it's always a treat to eat apples I've grown myself. But the blackberry season is already in full swing, even coming towards the end. Also, for foragers there are rosehips for rosehip syrup and sloes for sloe gin.

Some people, not directly tied to the seasons for their job, only see autumn as the beginning of winter. I beg to differ. To me, autumn is one of those seasons that, when the sun shines, can be much lovelier than any other season. Imagine walking on a sunny day in October as the low sun heightens the hues of the leaves as they drop and fall off the trees in a gentle spiral to carpet the ground. Or raking up the rich red leaves of a *Liquidambar styraciflua* or butter yellow leaves of *Ginkgo biloba* off a freshly green lawn.

Granted, there is more hope in spring because you have more to look forward to, but the key to autumn is to understand the beauty of transience: one day you can be admiring the leaves on the trees in the warm sunshine and the next you can be shivering by the fire with all the trees naked outside.

WANTING MORE:
BUYING, CHOOSING
AND GROWING YOUR OWN

Too Much on the Menu!

I once went to a garden centre in Essex that had the most dazzling array of plants available. Hundreds of perennial geraniums were stocked as well as some of the rarest and unusual shrubs. The problem was that rather like a restaurant with too much on the menu it was difficult to keep the plants from trying to escape from their pots.

What this meant in practical terms was that the plants for sale became increasingly root-bound and therefore did not establish nearly as well when planted. It is in the interests of both the garden centre and the customer that plants are bought soon after they are potted on (when the roots are just starting to peek through the holes at the bottom). Unfortunately, not every plant the garden centre stocks gets sold that quickly, if at all. Also, beware of newly potted on plants because you will be paying for compost instead of a bigger plant, which after all, is what you really want. I did hear a story from a fellow gardener about how he got a frightful ticking off because he was checking to see if the plants being sold had been newly potted on (which they probably had or they wouldn't have got so cross!).

There is also a question of definition here because strictly speaking garden centres only buy in plants, whereas nurseries mostly grow them themselves but sometimes also buy them in. Ideally, you want to buy from a nursery because the plants will be cheaper, possibly better quality and there will be a more interesting selection. This is not always the case but some nationwide chains have a tendency, in my humble opinion, to offer very poor value for money in all departments except in the virtue that they have a coffee shop on site.

My favourite nursery is in Ringstead, Norfolk where they

grow a lot of their own plants, such as wallflowers, cabbages and cucurbits. Also, you can hear the sound of church bells and the chirp of birds. It's a soothing, gentle place that seems to offer something more fulfilling than just a selection of plants. That is what retail nurseries offer in spades compared to your wholesaler, where the atmosphere is brisk and business-like. In a retail nursery you can ask questions about the suitability of plants without being told to get lost. However, as Christopher Lloyd said, do not ask the nurseryman endless questions about small purchases or he may be forced to chuck the whole thing in!

Buying plants in London is generally an expensive business and not one I would recommend, especially if you have the time and energy to go elsewhere. But there can be good deals to be had at market stalls and New Covent Garden Market.

Weed or Desirable Plant?

*I*t's always bizarre what people, including myself, will buy from the garden centre. The truth is that very little information is given about what a plant will be like. Most of the time a purchase is based on how pretty the flowers are without any consideration for the situation or the soil a plant may like or its vigour. So if I were to dig up the bindweed on my allotment and potted it up with a small picture of its white, piss-pot flowers (maybe I wouldn't use that term) and priced it at £6.95 stating *Vigorous, hardy perennial climber with beautiful pure white flowers,* how many people would buy it!?

Bargains and Thrown out Plants

*I*t's amazing the effect of reducing the price of plants can have on some people, no matter how small their garden and careful they are with their money. Even if the plant is still not particularly cheap and completely unsuitable for their garden because it's full shade and the plant is a sun-lover, they'll nonetheless insist on filling up the trolley. Honestly!

There is a client who loves rescuing plants that have been thrown out. It's really quite endearing — a bit like having a house full of rescued cats and dogs!

Invariably, these plants tend to sulk for a couple of years before we reluctantly give up on them. However, there was an occasion when she brought home a very sorry looking clematis (which I laughed at) and it turned out to thrive on a very unpromising wall with the most delicate purple flowers. So perhaps I should be more open to new experiences because there are always plenty of surprises in life, even on a subject that I am supposed to be 'an expert' in.

Propagation

I am not a great propagator much to my shame. But I am getting better! At one time I limited myself to digging up plants that had self-sown from another plant in the same garden. In fact, gravel is a superb habitat to have in a garden. So many different plants from your own and your neighbours' gardens pop up in it because its superb drainage stops seeds rotting. I had *Verbena bonariensis*, bedding pansies, polyanthus, *Aquilegia* spp., *Salvia sclarea* var. *turkestanica*, *Geranium sanguineum* and many others, which were all gratefully potted up and used elsewhere. This small patch of gravel was in an understanding neighbour's garden where I was paid to work but could also just pop in to do a few small things when I felt like. Sadly, as a professional gardener, I don't do much pottering around like this; you're always in a rush to get the job done. It's a shame because when I am gardening for someone else scarcely a day goes by when I don't find a *Cornus sanguinea* stem that has rooted and could be made into a separate plant, or a *Geranium phaeum* that has self-sown in a shady woodland garden or indeed a clump of snowdrops that could be split up.

My recent fad is hardwood cuttings. Since I have more time in early winter, I can make hardwood cuttings at my leisure and there are many plants, which can be propagated such as *Buddleja globosa*, roses, *Lonicera* × *purpusii* and the ornamental elders such as *Sambucus* 'Black Lace' to name but a few. If you have a large vegetable garden or allotment you can easily put some hardwood cuttings in (having improved the drainage with horticultural grit) and, apart from the occasional weeding, leave them to it. Admittedly , the success rate is not very high but not impossibly low either!

Plant Families and Their Cultivation

*W*hen I was at Hadlow College I had this exam question: *What are the similarities between the cultivation of plants in the same plant family?* It's a fascinating question because obviously plants in the same family are more closely linked genetically than ones that are not. So you would think that there would be some thread in the way to grow them.

For example, many of our brassicas originate from the bitter wildlings found in the cracks in cliffs. It's a remarkable journey for a vegetable to come from such humble beginnings to the plump heads of cabbage we have now. However, because of this ancient habitat of limestone cliffs most brassicas prefer a limey soil — this is why many allotmenteers add lime before growing brassicas.

In contrast, all plants in the *Ericaeae* demand an acidic soil (e.g. heathers (*Erica* spp.), *Skimmia japonica* and *Pieris japonica*). An exception to this common trait in the *Ericaeae* is that the strawberry tree (*Arbutus unedo*), which thrives on limestone soil. For example, it's found in the limestone mountains of the Cévennes in Southern France, combining beautifully with wild box (*Buxus sempervirens*), *Viburnum tinus*, old man's beard (*Clematis vitalba*), wild roses and actually the odd oak (*Quercus robur*).

In England, camellias are synonymous with Cornwall because its mild, damp climate is so ideal for their cultivation. Many of the big estates there have diverse collections of them often mixed with magnolias, rhododendrons and azaleas. This combination is supposed to be quite a breath-taking sight in early spring.

In fact because so many different types of Camellia were grown in Cornwall, the hybrid *Camellia × williamsii* (which tolerates the low light levels of England) was bred there in 1923.

Anyway, it was inevitable that some entrepreneurial type there would grow tea (*Camellia sinesis*) because it's a close relative of the ornamental camellia and apparently a blend is produced there containing some Cornish tea.

It's Like 10,000 Spades
When All You Need is a Fork

*I*rony is intertwined with gardening. Craving courgettes in my stir-fry, I duly bought some from the supermarket in mid-October thinking that my plants would not fruit again only to find that the last scraps of summer had produced a series of mini-courgettes on my plants, perfect for stir-frying. It is very similar with ornamental plants. No sooner have I bought a plant from the garden centre then I will have a visitor or a guest who will say, 'oh- but they grow like weeds in my garden!'.

It just seems that certain plants relish particular situations. There is no point fighting against nature. A garden on chalk planted up with rhododendrons is always going to end in tears because they need acidic soil. This is just another of those situations which confirms the expression *the grass is always greener on the other side of the fence*, because we always want what we cannot grow in our own garden.

This ties in with Beth Chatto's doctrine of always planting the right plant in the right place. She very modestly claimed that this was based on asking her husband about the native habitats of wild plants, which underestimates her own great skill of being able to place plants in the ideal position for them to thrive in such as in her famous dry garden in Essex.

GARDENING FROM AN ARMCHAIR

Uncle Monty's Firm, Ripe Carrot

*A*s Uncle Monty said in *Withnail and I*:

> I think the carrot infinitely more fascinating than the geranium. The carrot has mystery. Flowers are essentially tarts. Prostitutes for the bees. There is, you'll agree, a certain Je ne sais quoi – oh so very special – about a firm, young carrot!

I'm not sure I entirely agree with those sentiments but the carrot family is quite fascinating in its diversity! There is a wide array of wild plants in the *Apiaceae* family aside from the 'umbel carrot to the frothy blooms of cow parsley (*Anthriscus sylvestris*) that adorn the roadside to the red spotted stems of deadly hemlock (*Conium maculatum),* which was famously Socrates's last drink, to our native sea holly (*Eryngium maritimum*), which was candied and used in Elizabethan banquets. This diversity can even be drawn from European species or indeed the bare cupboard of British native flora.

The carrot family was one of the first to be classified because its distinctive flowers contain a simple or compound umbel (where the flower heads are of a uniform size and come from the same stalk). Because so many of the plants in this family look similar in their leaf form and flower shape it is easy to mistake the delicious from the deadly. This is why I never go foraging in the hedgerows for a bit of wild parsley; it's not worth taking the risk for 50 pence of herbs!

I Never Promised You a Rose Garden

*T*here is a book by this name about a young girl's struggle with schizophrenia — and very dark it is. But gardening has been proven to give a light at the end of the tunnel for many people affected by mental illness. I know this because that's exactly what happened to me as I discovered that life is more like Forrest Gump's box of chocolates, where you never know what you're going to get, rather than Amelie's hopeful image of people having orgasms from smelling a melon. Being paranoid that people are constantly talking about you, in a negative way, behind your back is not a delusion that goes away easily. But putting yourself in a non-confrontational setting with some gentle exercise thrown in can really be really helpful.

Gardening is often as close as many people get to their ancestral roots as hunter-gatherers or, more recently, as farmers. This is true not just for urban people but in many cases, those in the countryside too. Gardening tends to make people happier. Personally, even if you weren't mentally ill, I would recommend gardening as a stress reliever.

A British Obsession

*T*he British have a strong tradition of being good gardeners from Gertrude Jekyll to Vita Sackville-West to Dan Pearson. But looking through the train window onto suburban London, you wouldn't believe this to be the case: endless patios and unkempt grass. The truth is that most people turn to gardening in retirement because they have more leisure time, and gardening is a peaceful and healthy form of exercise. Different nations' attitudes to what they like to do in leisure time was summed up by Bill Bryson when he said, 'Germans have magazines devoted to sex in the same way that the British devote magazines to gardening.' It's quite an interesting thought that whilst an Englishman is pottering around his herbaceous border, his German counterpart is on a sun-lounger in Thailand.

The Gnome
and the Bouncing Bra-Line

*F*or those of us that were around in 90s, *Ground Force* was one of those programmes we all remember fondly. *Ground Force* was a programme that transformed neglected gardens from Aberdeen to Zennor. They always seemed to go to the most "underrated" places. Most famously, there was the braless Charlie Dimmock, whose oversized melons wobbled all over the place as she moved plants around the garden looking for a suitable spot for them. But it was her simple, girl-next-door charm that made her so appealing. This is one of the qualities of most gardeners: they are quite literally very down to earth.

Ground Force was also Alan Titchmarsh's big break and still his gnome-like face is all over the TV as a presenter. Indeed, he also presents a show on Classic FM because gardening and classical music do appeal to a certain generation. Tommy Walsh completed the trio with his cheeky humour and exceptional landscaping skills.

The difficulty with instant make overs where the tree ferns are wheeled out, the grass rolled out like a carpet and full-sized trees and shrubs planted is that they are expensive to create and very little thought is given to bringing the garden gently into maturity.

Most trees and shrubs take about three to five years to mature to full size. Groundcover plants take a similar amount of time to carpet areas and also herbaceous plants and grasses always look far more impressive after about three years. So invariably on *Ground Force* they plant everything too close together to create an instant effect and the plants grow into each other. Also, if you plant smaller plants they tend to establish more quickly and often overtake specimens that were bigger when they were planted. Finally, *Ground Force* inevitably happens in high summer and so these large plants all need copious amounts of water to survive during any hot weather before they get their roots down.

A classic example of this was one particular scene when they were looking to quickly cover an ugly garden shed at the bottom of the garden. Alan Titchmarsh suggested they use a Russian vine (*Fallopia baldschuanica*). This is an extremely fast-growing climber nicknamed 'Mile a Minute'. To speed things along even further they mulched it with well-rotted horse manure. I'm sure it covered the shed very quickly! But once the cameras had left and the poor owner of the garden was left to deal with it, there would have been more than a few muttered curse-words as it took over the bottom of the garden by sending out shoots willy-nilly in every direction like some unhinged, giant triffid!

Alan Titchmarsh's Garden Nightmares

*W*hen I was at horticultural college one of the running jokes was about a lecturer who had a small nursery on top of his lecturing duties. Because he had become overloaded with work at the college, let's just say the garden centre had somewhat gone to seed. We used to say it would have been a good candidate for the garden version of Gordon Ramsey's *Kitchen Nightmares,* in which an experienced gardener, such as Alan Titchmarsh, would go round various horticultural businesses telling them where they had gone wrong. I'm not sure if dear old Alan Titchmarsh would use the f-word quite as readily as Gordon Ramsay, but you never know, eh?

THE ROMANCE
OF THE ENGLISH COUNTRYSIDE

Blackbirds

I think most people have a great fondness for the blackbird. And it's reciprocated. By bird standards, they are quite affectionate and of course sing beautifully. Richard Mabey summed their contribution perfectly when he said, 'It's mid-April and the first day warm enough to have a cup of tea with the back door open. The smell of lilac drifts in whilst the blackbird sings a song so reflective and relaxed that it captures the whole aura of the evening.'

In my previous garden there was a topiary yew that was about 12 foot tall, which our local blackbird used to hide under and gorge on the berries. It liked to relieve itself on the other side of the garden under the buddleia. I know this because I would see it skulking there and gradually a whole miniature forest of yew seedlings emerged — much to my delight. You notice such tiny details when you spend hours in a small garden. As a footnote to this: yew seeds need scarification to germinate. This is the process by which a seed coat is damaged, by various different means, to allow the cotyledon to germinate. Astonishingly, scarification can be provided by a bird's stomach.

Anyway, we dug up these seedlings and planted them in memory of my father at my parent's house in Norfolk after he died in 2009, aged 62. His yews, I am pleased to say, are now three foot tall and very happy. Such satisfaction can be achieved by such small pleasures. Whether our yew will last as long as the oldest yew tree in Britain seems unlikely as 3,000 years is a long time. This is apparently how old the Fortingall yew is, found in a churchyard in Perthshire, Scotland! However, there is a yew tree that has been turned into a chapel in Normandy, France and the thought of that happening to my dad's yew tree does appeal to me very much...

Stalls

I love plant stalls and by that I mean informal stalls outside little cottages in the countryside. I suppose like most people, I love the idea of a bargain and certainly the plants on them are unlikely to be even half the price of the same plant in a garden centre. That is hardly surprising because the plants probably propagated themselves in the owner's garden. Anyway, it's nice to have some remnants of a rural economy when you can buy eggs, honey, plants and cut flowers from a cottage by the side of the road. It's got a certain whiff of entrepreneurship about it, but perhaps more in the spirit of Pop Larkin from *The Darling Buds of May* than Gordon Gekko from the film *Wall Street*.

Good plants to buy from plant stalls are aquilegias (*Aquilegia* spp.), although you won't know what colour they are (because they are quite promiscuous and so the colour varies a lot); the spider plant (*Chlorophytum comosum*), an easy to grow houseplant; perennial geraniums or maybe bear's breeches (*Acanthus mollis*), if your chosen cottager can make root cuttings. Just remember that if you don't have the exact change don't short-change them when you put the money in the box...

Rain

*I*n England we have different types of rain because it rains so much. Since we are so obsessed with our weather we have almost as many terms for different types of rain as the French do, in their much loved cuisine, for different types of simmering water.

Here I describe the different grades of rain according to my own experience as a gardener. Lowest down the scale is when it is spitting. This hardly counts as rain at all because you hardly get wet even if you aren't wearing a raincoat. Gardeners who don't work in this type of rain should just find a new profession because they won't make enough money to wash their face.

Next up the scale is a light drizzle. Very similar to cricket, when gardening in this weather you grit your teeth and carry on in the hope that it is just a passing shower. It is not a pleasant experience but as long as it's not winter drizzle you should be alright.

The real problem arises when the light drizzle turns to a heavy drizzle. This is the point when the covers are brought on in cricket or the gardener decides not to tread on the beds because he will do more harm than good and takes shelter under a large tree.

Next up the scale is heavy rain. There is a gardener of my acquaintance who loves nothing better than to work in warm summer rain. You get drenched but apparently there is something deeply poetic and cleansing about gardening in this type of rain, a bit like swimming in the Ganges.

Top of the scale is the thunderstorm. Obviously, in this weather gardening or indeed standing under a tree is extremely unwise but maybe there are some macho gardeners out there that get a thrill out of it. For me it is best to retreat inside and drink a cup of sweet milky tea! I always associate thunderstorms in England with June because that is when the weather changes from cold to humid but I'm sure July and August must have their fair share of thunderstorms too.

Alastair and the Geese

*A*t my parent's house in Norfolk we have a field at the back on which geese graze. They look straight out of an impressionist painting. However, rather like doves in a dovecote, the image is rather less pleasant than the reality. The doves were evicted from the dovecote by the rooks and took up residence in our courtyard breeding, and not surprisingly, shitting everywhere. The geese don't breed as fast but they can make a lawn a serious health hazard if you let them spend too much time on it.

My father decided one day that he had had enough. So he took my air-pistol and chased the geese off the field. Unfortunately, a passing rambler saw him (or was it the local busybody?) and reported to the local police that there was a madman with pure white hair waving a gun about in Old Hunstanton. This being Norfolk, a policeman came round and made some very gentle enquiries in his thick Norfolk accent about the incident. However, they ended up joking and smiling about it very quickly and, not surprisingly, nothing came of it. Perhaps things might be different today with the advent of Islamic State and Britain First.

Woodlands

*P*lants from woodlands are some of the most beautiful in the world and as much as I would like to say that British woodlands are the best, I'm afraid that is not true. The woodlands of North America and China take some beating in that regard. Nevertheless, there is something special about a wood of bluebells (*Hyacinthoides non-scripta*), wild garlic (*Allium ursinum*) or wood anemones *(Anemone nemorosa).* Because of their familiarity, they always evoke happy memories of good times in the British nature lover, perhaps when listening to the sound of the cuckoo under a secluded oak with a lover lying next to you in the dappled shade. Unfortunately, that reference is not based on personal experience!

The thing I like best about woodland, particularly deciduous woodland, is the dappling of sunlight in the wood. It emphasizes the transience of the seasons because the lighting varies as the sun moves across the sky, creating thousands if not millions of patterns on the woodland floor.

A Realist's Lawn

*T*he lawn is ubiquitous with an English garden thanks to the large amount of rainfall we have. On the continent the lawns are very inferior. In fact, they really just have grass. That's my line anyway and I won't change it unless Ms Merkel sends her tanks onto my lawn.

I am not obsessed with having a perfect lawn but I have to admit, watching the Teutonic determination of a groundsman as he mows the lawn in dead straight lines is very satisfying. Also as weeds, particularly dandelions, seem determined to squeeze into my lawns at every opportunity (how *do* they germinate with no bare earth?), I do use 'weed 'n feed'. But I do so with a heavy heart, similar to the guilty frustration with which I spread slug pellets following an attack on my precious vegetables or bedding.

Mowing the lawn is one of those jobs you do to relax but relaxing is of course meant relatively here. It's not as relaxing as drinking rum punch on a deck chair in the Caribbean, for example. It's satisfying and not too much hard work, provided you have a mower suitable to the size of your lawn. I use an electric mower because I am not at all mechanically minded. The only thing I have to worry about is not mowing over the cord provided it's already assembled like a Flymo. There was an unfortunate incident when I tried to assemble a mower and every time I tried to mow the lawn, bits fell off it. Not very professional but luckily my clients never saw, so it's alright!

A FORAY INTO FUNGI

Mycorrhizae

*W*e obviously rely on fungi to break down organic matter, most notably in the garden and woods. But mycorrhizae are a specific type of fungus that we heavily rely on in order to increase the yield and performance of our horticultural crops and ornamentals.

How it works is that the roots of a plant form a partnership (or symbiotic relationship) with mycorrhizae to increase the surface area of the plant's root system, thereby increasing its intake of important nutrients such as potassium or phosphorus from the soil. In return for forming this partnership, the mycorrhizae receive sugars from the plant's roots, which the plant has transported from its leaves following its production there by photosynthesis.

For a while, Monty Don used a mycorrhizae on Gardener's World that you could buy and apply to the roots of newly planted trees and shrubs but I think there is still much debate over whether or not it worked, or rather how effective it really is for the price. I was always told to add bone meal in the autumn because it aids root growth but that has also been questioned.

At the end of the day, the bigger the hole you make and the more organic matter (such as well-rotted manure or leaf mould) you stuff into that hole, the better the start most plants will have. And any additional concoctions you add such as mycorrhizae will do no harm and probably even do some good provided you follow the instructions on the packet!

Foraging

*S*earching for wild food is something that comes naturally to humans and is very satisfying. The problem is that most people don't have the knowledge to identify plants and therefore are quite rightly suspicious. I'm not sure if celebrity chefs really help matters. I once watched Hugh Fearnley-Whittingstall in *A Cook on the Wild Side* serve up deep fried minnows and steamed hogweed shoots washed down with parsnip wine to one befuddled Welshman.

Exaggerating the palatability of certain wild plants does not really encourage people to eat wild foods if they taste awful. However, there are some wild foods that will taste better than any cultivated vegetable that you are likely to taste, e.g. wild garlic (*Allium ursinum*), marsh samphire (*Salicornia europaea*), wild plums (*Prunus* spp.) and ceps (*Boletus edulis*).

Having tasted plants such as Alexanders (*Smyrnium olusatrum*) and garlic mustard (*Alliaria petiolata*), which were apparently used as potherbs in Medieval Times, it occurs to me how desperate these people must have been to eat such things and how lucky I am to be able to buy a cappuccino or a curry without having to resort to eating plants that taste so bitter that you immediately spit them out!

A classic example of this amongst potherbs is Tansy (*Tanacetum vulgare*), which was the most grown herb in Medieval Times because of its anthelmintic properties. The reason it is so good at dispelling worms is because it is slightly poisonous and also quite bitter. Hence when food hygiene standards were improved, it was quietly moved to the Ye Olde Herbe Garden and there it will remain, I sincerely hope!

The Magic of Mushrooms

I have already talked about foraging but mushrooms are perhaps worth a separate mention. It was not so long ago that you could buy magic mushrooms fresh in the shops. I can remember my fellow students at Leeds University in 2004 could not believe their luck at the availability of such things at the local shop. The law was quickly reversed after that — much to the disappointment of students and hippies up and down the land!

As a reaction to this, quasi-headshops in Camden started selling fly agaric (*Amanita muscaria*) (the original toadstool but without the attached fairy). It wasn't illegal to sell because the government quite rightly assumed that no one would be stupid enough to eat it! I should clarify here that it is not deadly poisonous but the effects can be unpleasant. The Lapps apparently found a more delicious way of consuming fly agaric by drinking reindeer piss (which has traces of the mushroom in it because the reindeer browse on fly agarics). One of the side effects is it makes the user take gigantic leaps over tiny objects. So you can imagine Goths in Camden taking huge leaps over the cracks in the paving.

To more savoury and palatable subjects: I used to go hunting for ceps (*Boletus edulis*) in October. The time to go was when there was a full moon and ideally a dry spell followed by rain. The good thing about the Boletus family is that they are easily identified by their spongy gills on the underside of the cap. Happily, no mushroom in that family is deadly poisonous unlike other mushroom families such as the Amanita. Having said that, the Devil's boletus (*Rubroboletus satanas)* will give you a very bad stomach ache so always check in a reliable book such as Peter Jordan's *New Guide to Mushrooms* or Roger Phillip's *Mushrooms*. My favourite way to eat them is fried with garlic in butter and then mixed with cream and parsley before tossing them in spaghetti. However, mushrooms on toast is a classic and I have happy memories of the smells of moss and pine as we found and then ate chanterelles (*Cantharellus cibarius*) on toast in southern Scotland.

The giant puffball (*Calvatia gigantea*) is a similar treat but I rarely see it these days. Be careful when picking field mushrooms (*Agaricus campestris*). The yellowstainer (*Agaricus xanthodermus*) is easy to miss and it will make you very sick if you eat it. It looks exactly like a field mushroom but has yellow stains on the stem. Anyway, mushrooms are a fascinating subject and everyone should explore them more deeply rather than just buying chestnut mushrooms in little sealed packets.

Ray Mears's Mate

*W*hen Ray Mears was doing his programme on wild food he had a very eccentric scientist called Gordon as co-presenter. It always seemed to fall to Gordon to try Ray's foraged food, poor bugger. He would nibble on it, a bit like a rabbit, and tactfully say, 'It's a bit bitter isn't it.' Probably, immediately afterwards, they would be forced to switch off the camera so he could spit out the offending object and wash his mouth out!

Gordon did however recount the funniest story of a scientific cock-up. Apparently a friend of his used to collect mushrooms for examination, dissection etc. And he'd usually take the edible species home to eat. A mistake was made and he took the poisonous species home by accident. Realizing what had happened he put a Post-it note of the exact species name on his shirt just before he was carted off to A&E. I can't imagine the looks on the nurses' faces as they wheeled him into the operating theatre! It's difficult to understand how on the one hand he knew the exact species of mushroom but on the other made the assumption that it was edible. Gordon told this story with such a straight face it was difficult to stop myself shrieking with laughter as I watched it. I should hasten to add that I think his friend was okay and does not need regular dialysis, thanks to an early identification of the species which poisoned him.

THE GARDENER'S STOMACH

The Feminist Beekeepers Association

I have never kept bees and I doubt I ever will. However, I have had various experiences of the advantages and disadvantages of beekeeping. I have tasted the Grand Cru of British honey given to me by the ever-generous Ted and Nettie, Essex beekeepers extraordinaire. Lathered on crumpets with lashings of butter, it made teatime something very special.

I have also been dive-bombed by bees whilst working at a community garden in London. They'd been provoked by anti-social behaviour in the garden and even though they did not actually sting, this didn't make the wild dash away from the hive any more pleasant.

Finally, there was the time I went on a day course that introduced beekeeping. The beekeeper was a massive feminist and kept on comparing the role of drones (male bees) in the hive to men hanging about the pub drinking pissy lager on tap while looking for a quickie. I often wondered whether there was a meeting of the 'Feminist Beekeepers' in Totnes or some such place where they stripped naked and danced round the bonfire drinking mead...

Allotments

The thing I like best about going to my allotment is seeing so many friendly faces — a welcome relief in London! The thing I like least is all the bloody weeding. Obviously, if you leave a patch of ground bare then very quickly certain types of plant will find ways of colonizing it and with so much bare earth on an allotment this is what happens. The effect on my attitude to horticulture has been two-fold.

Firstly, I have become a lot more interested in permaculture because, if used correctly, mulches and green manures, for example, can reduce the workload whilst increasing fertility.

Secondly, I have to say that I no longer believe that organic agriculture is anything other than a niche market. This is because if I can't manage my tiny allotment without slug pellets and Roundup how on earth is a farmer with a thousand acre farm going to manage without chemicals? Not very well! Indeed, it sounds like a recipe for disaster! In regard to this I do sometimes wonder whether my definition of organic is the same as those who sell many food products labelled as organic.

Regardless, I would say that a lot more research could go into the study of companion planting and permaculture techniques instead of it being left to the vague mysticism of the hippies.

Of course the original reason I got an allotment was to eat really delicious food. As already stated, you cannot beat fresh produce in terms of taste.

Having an abundance of fresh vegetables has also made me realize how much I had limited my cooking to the consumption of meat. In fact, as people always say, with really good vegetarian food you don't miss the meat and frankly my health has benefited from not being such a committed sausage muncher.

The vegetable that I have eaten the most of since my acquisition of an allotment is Swiss chard. It grows like a weed on the London clay in Brixton to such an extent that it is a deadly insult on our allotment site to offer it to anyone there. This is ironic since most people adore it. This is partly because it doesn't store well and so is not readily available in the supermarket. It's also a very versatile vegetable, much prized in France and the Middle East, with its green leaves and white stems offering two very different vegetables for the price of one.

Companion Planting

*C*ompanion planting is the process by which two plants can be grown together with mutually beneficial results. Therefore, it is much used in the production of vegetables, especially in small-scale organic situations.

Obviously, it is not the same as ivy climbing a tree or indeed the parasitic mistletoe growing in apple tops. The classic example of superb companion planting is the Three Sisters, where sweet corn, pumpkins and runner beans were simultaneously grown together by the American Indians. They aided each other by providing support in different mutually beneficial ways: the pumpkins suppress the weeds, the runner beans fix nitrogen into the soil for the pumpkins and the sweet corn supports the runner beans. Actually, the Three Sisters aren't such great companions here in Britain because the runner beans outcompete the sweet corn due to the additional moisture in the British climate.

What is better known is that certain plants produce chemicals thought to actively repel or suppress either pests or weeds that may affect one of the companion plants. For example, it is often stated, without much scientific evidence, that marigolds repel whitefly on greenhouse tomatoes.

This is not the same as allelopathy, where chemicals released by a plant seem to indiscriminately kill any species within a certain area. For example, the black walnut releases a toxin from its roots called juglone and the needles from many pine trees release a compound which inhibits the growth of other species they come into contact with under the canopy.

Companion planting can sometimes take the form of one plant, such as an apple tree, offering shade to something like lettuce, which would bolt more easily if exposed to full sun on a hot day.

To find out more about the best associations to use on a vegetable plot, I would recommend Gertrud Franck's book, *Companion Planting*, which gives detailed lists and drawings of rotations. From my own studies, I know that marigolds have proved an effective green manure to use before a crop susceptible to nematode attack is planted, such as strawberries, bulbs or potatoes. In fact, an American company called Burpee sells a marigold seed called 'Nema-Gone', which would presumably be used for this very purpose.

Lavender Fudge

*T*he first summer I started studying as a horticulturalist, I got a summer job at Norfolk Lavender. I have to say it was quite boring, menial work except when we used the still to produce lavender essential oil (I was not senior enough to operate it although I did watch it being used). Like so many rural jobs, the romance of working on a sort of farm (although it was a tourist attraction too) was not all it was cracked up to be. But there was one funny moment that I still remember: we were cutting the beech hedge near the shop when one of the retail assistants offered us some fudge that was about to go off. It seemed too good an offer so we gratefully accepted the mixed bag of fudge. As we munched, the head gardener's face screwed up in disgust. 'I would have to get lavender flavour, wouldn't I?!' Having spent years rubbing against the lavender plants in the garden and stinking of lavender, the last thing he wanted was the taste of it in his mouth as well!

Pumpkins

*O*ne of my favourite childhood books was *The Mystery of the Enormous Pumpkin*. It involved two mice, I think, watering a single pumpkin so it grew to the size of ... I don't know what. Perhaps a gilded carriage to carry a princess? It stirred the fascination I had with vegetables, particularly enormous ones. I am relieved to say that this obsession with large vegetables did not transfer into adulthood because I do not have the talent or single mindedness to spend all summer nurturing 6 foot long runner beans for a prize of 79 pence!

This was also the era of the cult children's film *Honey I Shrunk the Kids* that made me appreciate that even our immediate world can be a fantastic and mysterious place. Later, I was to revisit this theme when I watched Robert MacFarlane's *The Wild Places of Essex*. In this four-part BBC series, he takes the viewer to a variety of places where the natural world inspired him, from Billericay to Basildon, in spite of the encroachments of man and industry. He had to deal with a lot of cynicism; Essex becomes less and less like the land of the snow goose every day! As one person sarcastically replied to him, 'You want to find the wild places of Essex? Well, you better get down Basildon High Street on a Saturday night!'

WEEDS, BEASTIES AND COWBOYS

London Pests

*C*ity-dwellers really have very little idea of the effect living in a city can have on decreasing the number of mammals preying on their plants. Rabbits and deer are such a big problem as browsers of plants in the countryside. But, those animals able to co-exist with human beings really seem to thrive in cities, however.

The fox, for example, seems to be skulking on every street corner eating discarded fried chicken bones. I've had the misfortune of finding a few treats that foxes have buried in my clients' gardens including a used nappy and a packet of rotting bacon. When I mentioned this to a client they suggested that perhaps they were saving these treats for some kind of birthday celebration!

Pigeons also go feral in London and love nothing better than pointlessly pecking cigarette butts. Perhaps the Jonathan Livingston Seagull types are a bit more adventurous, flying out to suburban allotments to feast on brassicas.

Squirrels have proliferated into any area with trees and seem to spend a huge amount of time digging up the lawn to look for nuts, stealing your precious tulip or crocus bulbs and fighting with each other for territory. It's interesting that my local squirrels in Dulwich seem to have retained more of the red of our native squirrel. This makes me wonder if the Dulwich hills were perhaps a stronghold for the red squirrel once upon a time, when The Great North Wood stretched from Deptford to Crystal Palace. Sadly, there is more fantasy than truth in this daydream!

A more recent development (possibly thanks to climate change) is the spread in south London of the parakeet, which seems to be beating our native birds to the available food. On a mild December day, I was playing tennis in Dulwich Park as the sunset went a deep orange tinged with pink and the parakeets squawked in the eucalyptus trees. It was so warm and pleasant I thought I'd been transported to the Orient.

The Box Tree Caterpillar

*W*e recently had an outbreak of a new pest in London called the box tree caterpillar, which devastated the box plants (*Buxus Sempervirens)* of Clapham, Chelsea and Battersea, in particular.

Rapidly, all the box plants of my clients' gardens were defoliated by this naughty pest, much to their annoyance. Actually, the moth that lays the eggs is very attractive and exotic looking (it's from Asia) but the caterpillars, in green and black, look like they're from outer space.

I was desperately trying to stop their advance by spraying them with a pyrethrum-based pesticide (please forgive me, Bob Flowerdew!). But they would not get the message and kept re-appearing and munching until I was forced to remove the poor box hedge.

'That's the end of them, now,' I thought as the defoliated box plants sat neatly packed away in green bags in the back of my van.

A few minutes later I got the distinctly unpleasant feeling of the little blighters climbing up my legs in the driver's seat as I crossed Clapham High Street. I had to step on the pavement and reach up my trousers to peel them off my legs, much to the interest of the passers-by. All I was thinking of was the scene of Mowgli in *Jungle Book* when he is surrounded by snakes desperately saying the master words, 'We be of one blood, ye and I.'

I am not sure a master word would have worked with these insects; they were too persistent and stupid! Whilst grinding them into the pavement all I was thinking was, I can see how you made it here from Asia! If only there was a swarm of blackbirds to give you and all your extended family a good seeing to, I would be happy!'

Sweet Talking

When I worked in a garden centre in London, I met a colleague who was keen to tell me how he used to charm his customers with his 'sweet-talk' as he was a proper London geezer. His comments went something like this: 'Yeah, sweet-talk 'em, mate! You know what I mean ... sure I'll have a cuppa tea no problem ... and if you don't nick anything so much the better!'

A similar situation of sweet-talking occurred when I was away from a client's garden for a year. A new gardener had wormed his way in and persuaded her that a love of flame colours (which she claimed to have) included the colour blue. Technically he was right – a flame can have blue in it – but in terms of which colours are in the same grouping on the colour wheel, he was stretching the truth somewhat!

Not all gardeners are like this but since there is no real universal qualification like the BALI registration for landscapers it's easy for the sweet talkers, bull-shitters and cowboys to slip through the net. Obviously, a horticultural qualification is great but in most cases many gardeners, some of them very good, don't have any certificates — just years of experience and observation.

The best bit of sweet-talking I did was to suggest that a client's rockery filled with evergreen conifers was the sort of low maintenance planting appropriate for a school of nit-wits. A rip-off from Christopher Lloyd but true!

Lovin' a Cold Climate

*T*here are times of year when gardening can be extremely hard work, for instance when the changeable British climate is in a bad mood! An example of this is when the wind has whipped up and is blowing leaves all around the garden in the light drizzle of late autumn. Raking leaves up in that sort of weather is very time consuming and not very efficient but has to be done because you cannot take too many days off in the autumn for wind or rain or you would hardly work at all.

The other difficult scenario in gardening that springs to mind is weeding the garden in mid-February. As the amount of light per day increases, many of the annual weeds start to germinate and then grow very slowly. The one that seems most common in the gardens I look after is bittercress (*Cardamine hirsuta*). This plant self-seeds very readily once it gets going so it's better to get it early. This means getting cold fingers as you carefully winkle out the tiny seedlings before they have time to flower and reproduce in late winter.

However, I think one misconception that people have about the climate in Britain when they work in offices is that the climate of Mediterranean regions of the world (South of France, California, Greece, etc.) is vastly superior. What they overlook is that for large portions of the year the weather is unbearably hot outside and so manual work or indeed any exercise is extremely tiring. They don't notice this because the ice cubes are clinking in their Aperol as they sit on terrace in the shade of a vine covered pergola! What I am saying is that the great virtue of the British weather, despite prolonged periods of rain and relative cold, is that it is moderate. We rarely get excessively cold or hot weather and that is why we are a nation of gardeners, which is why I love our climate despite its seeming faults.

EXOTIC INFLUENCES
FROM FURTHER AFIELD

❧

My Bucket List

I worked at Kirstenbosch Botanical Gardens in Cape Town as a volunteer. And very interesting it was too. However, I didn't go to Cape Town just to see the plants; it was also to escape the severe mental challenge that an English winter presents to us all. People deal with it in different ways: some devour books, some drink and some, like me, simply despair. As my aunt lived in Cape Town, and had made an open-ended invitation that I could stay with her, there seemed to be a solution for that winter, at least. Namely, to fly south with the swallows...

As I visited during January, all the spring flowers were finished — which is what I'd expected. However, if I'd climbed the mountains around Cape Town with my aunt, I would have caught the famous and retiring *Disa uniflora*. But no such luck. I am not an early riser; she gets up at 5am despite being retired! Also, I was slightly concerned by her descriptions of the deadly puff-adder hiding on stones on the foot-path and preying on unsuspecting walkers.

However, I did see many king proteas (*Protea cynaroides*) in flower (the national flower of South Africa), which was nice but hardly impressive as they grew all through the golf course and gated community I was staying on.

The most amusing thing about working at Kirstenbosch was that on my first day, without any introduction, I was set to work weeding the endangered plants garden on my own. Not being familiar with South African flora, could I really be responsible for the extinction of a species? ... No, of course not! They had stock beds at the back of the garden where they had probably built up quite a number of reserves of the endangered plants I was weeding. But nevertheless, it was a strange introduction to gardening in South Africa!

Also, having grown up with British health and safety procedures (which I had always talked about with curled lip) it was disconcerting to have no warnings of possible hazards, such as snakes or creepy crawlies.

I hope to visit all the Mediterranean regions of the world before I die because they have the most diverse flora. I already have southern Europe and the Cape ticked off. Hopefully, I will also see the areas that haven't yet been turned into vineyards around Perth, Australia, but also visit California with its tree lupins (*Lupinus arboreus*), Californian poppies (*Eschscholzia californica*) and *Ceanothus* spp. Also, I would love to travel around that fascinating area of Chile, which has a Mediterranean climate but is slightly different because it's sandwiched between the mountains and the sea in a relatively small distance. This creates an interesting combination of maritime and alpine influence on the types of plants that grow there. It is possible that this makes the flora in Chile the most unusual out of all the Mediterranean regions.

Orchids

*W*hen I was at Hadlow College in Kent we went on some amazing field trips, such as to a Chinese man who supplied the Chinese greens to Chinatown in London. He used an organic method of growing the plants in slightly flooded soil so that frogs could thrive in the water channels between the crops and eat the slugs and snails that tried to nibble the plants (apparently it's a classic Oriental technique for growing Chinese greens).

But by far the best trip was when we went to an orchid meadow in Kent. With the buttercups and light pink of the lady orchids (*Orchis purpurea*) shimmering in one of those perfect early summer afternoons, it was one of those days I shall not forget in a hurry and enthused me with a passion for horticulture which I still have today.

Orchids have some lovely shapes from the bee orchid (*Ophrys apifera)* that looks like a bee to the orchid that looks like a lady's slipper (*Cypripedium calceolus)* or indeed the orchid that looks like a cut out of Arthur Conan Doyle's dancing men (*Orchis italica*). It really does feel like their creator was being very playful in how he (or she!) connected the shape of the orchid flower to other existing organisms. Of course, the bee orchid is a very clever evolutionary adaptation but with such variety in the shapes available it does seem to vindicate some sort of intelligent design theory although obviously orchid flowers are not quite as complex in design as the human eye.

Coastal Gardens

*O*ne of my favourite walks is through Whitstable towards Seasalter along the beach. Initially, there are big piles of empty oyster shells and fish sheds selling 'Fruits de Mer' types of shellfish. Then you notice the strong wind blowing salty fresh air into your face and then the not particularly attractive bay whose water is neither crystal clear nor its sand purest white. Being an estuary however, it's ideal for producing oysters. Then you notice the effects of gentrification where little fisherman's gardens have been tarted up by second-homers or DFLs (down from London) as they say. Anyway, I don't think anyone can complain about the state of their gardens. Often with some blue or grey paint, a *Phormium tenax* or *Agapanthus* spp., a lavender hedge or a spattering of *Verbena bonariensis* and some tastefully arranged stones or driftwood they often look very attractive, these coastal gardens.

Following this, there is an ever-so-sweet little pub with wooden boards selling Shepherd Neame ales. And finally, there's a more deserted area as you move away from Whitstable where dog roses have colonized in-land and mayweed (*Anthemis* spp.), red valerian (*Centranthus ruber*), yellow horned poppy (*Glaucium flavum*), sea kale (*Crambe maritima*) and mallows (*Malva sylvestris*) have managed to grow in what presumably are quite inhospitable conditions on the beach. Because of these things and the antique shops, the smell of fish and chips and the availability of local fruit in their greengrocers (particularly cherries in July!), I always relish these trips to the Kentish seaside in the balmy days of late summer.

The Dales

*T*o me, the real garden of England is the Yorkshire Dales in summer (although it can be a bit bleak for the rest of the year). There are various reasons for this but firstly because it rains so much the landscape is so verdantly green. Second, the dry stonewalls, babbling brooks and fluffy sheep create a scene so rural that I dream about it when in the Big Smoke. Finally, there is the limestone soil, which is the ideal medium for wildflowers to grow in to complete the effect. My favourites are *Geranium pratense*, buttercups (*Ranunculus* spp.) and pink campion (*Silene dioica*), which take on an ethereal quality in the white nights of June. The fact that such a landscape exists is due to a tenacity of spirit in Yorkshire folk, from whom we pansy southerners could learn a thing or two.

The Ribblehead viaduct in the Yorkshire Dales

🌜

A Walk from Hell

I have a special affection for Blythburgh Church, near Southwold. Despite having closer ties to Norfolk with its plethora of medieval churches, Blythburgh church is my favourite — and it's in Suffolk no less. Its chief quality is that it retains its medieval features because it was not viciously remodelled in Victorian times.

I decided to visit this church by public transport and a quick internet search produced a website claiming you could walk to the church from Halesworth, which has a railway station, along the River Blyth. What a good idea (I thought) and duly bought the tickets.

The day was bright and fresh and I set off in a good mood. After a lengthy journey to get to Halesworth, I arrived and located the river. A tarmac footpath followed it for a bit but when it divided the path became increasing overgrown with hemlock, which unnerved me as it is deadly poisonous and stinging nettles, which repeatedly stung my bare legs. I trudged on until I reached Blyford and saw another footpath leading along the river, which I took only to discover this was also overgrown with stinging nettles and worse still, giant hogweed. I tried not to touch the latter but must have brushed it because later I got some nasty blisters. However, what I got was nothing compared to the pictures on the internet of the effects on other people who touched it (not recommended viewing for the squeamish!).

Eventually I conceded defeat and – having muddied my shoes and jumped a farmer's gate – arrived somewhat fortuitously at a pub. As I drunk my pint, the rain came down hard. Perhaps a less stubborn person would have ordered a taxi and tucked into the lobster thermidor on the menu, but driving around Suffolk and eating vastly overpriced food is not what I consider an enjoyable day-out in the countryside. So I left and got soaked, temporarily lost in a field containing a nasty looking bull and then stung all over again before arriving bedraggled and quite wild back in Halesworth.

Much like in *Three Men in a Boat* by Jerome K. Jerome, I escaped the rain by taking the train to London. Never again did I think, whilst walking in heavy rain, that 'nature was beautiful, even in her tears', as he wryly commented during another downpour over their boat. Digressing slightly, I think the final scene of that book does seem to be a fair description of how many British holidays/trips seem to end when the heavens open:

Twenty minutes later, three figures, followed by a shame-faced looking dog, might have been seen creeping stealthily ... towards the railway station ... We reached Paddington at seven, and drove direct to the restaurant ... the odour of Burgundy, and French sauces knocked as a very welcome visitor ... 'Well' said Harris. 'We have had a pleasant trip ... but I think we did well to chuck it when we did. Here's to Three Men well out of a Boat!'

MY FAVOURITE
FAMOUS GARDENS

Charleston

*C*harleston is the house used by the Bloomsbury Set (a group of artists and writers including Virginia Woolf, Duncan Grant and Vanessa Bell) in the early part of the 20th century, which is in Sussex near Lewes. Famously, its members were constantly playing a game of musical beds. That is quite amusing of course but the reason I went was because I wanted to see the garden (and to a lesser extent the house), which is full of artistic and naturalistic free-thinking. It is in some respects a classic cottage garden with *Euphorbia characias subsp. wulfenii*, roses, hollyhocks, sweet peas and sunflowers. It probably looked a lot nicer when I saw it in 2010 than when the Bloomsbury Set was in residence. One suspects they may have been a bit lax on the weeding!

The problem for gardeners of historic houses is that they often feel constrained to achieve an authentic impression of what the garden would have looked like in its heyday. I actually don't think any gardener should try and re-create a garden in the exact image of say a picture of a garden from that era.

What they should say is that the garden is inspired by the spirit of the Bloomsbury Set, like a Hollywood film is inspired by true events rather than based on them.

East Ruston

*W*ithout doubt this is the best garden in Norfolk — and remember, Norfolk is a county of gardeners. Invariably, I am driving up to Norfolk on a Saturday and listening to "The Garden Party" on Radio Norfolk where Alan Gray, the owner of East Ruston Vicarage Gardens, is giving sound advice on gardening and bitching about other better-known gardeners. Also, it always seems that the Canaries (Norwich City football team) are always being thumped whenever I am listening to Radio Norfolk!

East Ruston Gardens is right in the most inaccessible corner of Norfolk and used to be open only from 2 to 5pm on Wednesdays, Saturdays and Sundays. This has now changed to more flexible hours and days, though, because of the sheer scale and impressiveness of the garden. Anyway, it requires a lot of effort to get there from most places even within the same county. It's worth it though: a series of different garden rooms beautifully furnished with plants, an unusual desert garden and views of two medieval churches on each side. I should go back next summer not least to see one of the owners directing traffic in the car park in his sailor-boy outfit!

The Smell of Turkish Delight
at The Chelsea Physic Garden

*W*hen I worked as a volunteer at the Chelsea Physic Garden, one of the first jobs they gave me was to take cuttings of their collection of pelargoniums. I found it quite an eye-opener or a scent-sation! 'Attar of Roses' was my favourite, reminding me of the rare occasions I have eaten real Turkish delight with it rose flavour and scent infused into the icing sugar. But there were other scents too such as orange, old spice, peppermint and other smells I could not name but seemed somehow familiar.

Eating roses has always seemed a very sensual act to me. Having watched *Like Water for Chocolate,* I sought out rose-petal jam, sold on Edgware Road, and then made Tita's famous dish of 'Quail with Rose-Petal Sauce' for dinner. Luckily, it did not have the same erotic effect on my family!

The romance of food makes me think of the BBC production of *Brideshead Revisited* where Sebastian Flyte and Charles Ryder share a box of strawberries and a bottle of Chateau Peryraguey under an oak tree on a cloudless day in June. You could not hope for a better love letter to the English countryside than that.

Exotic gardens

*C*hristopher Lloyd, the great 20th century gardener, popularized the idea of an exotic garden in the same way that Elizabeth David, the great 20th century food writer, popularized the use of olive oil. What I mean is that the concepts did exist before they starting banging their drums about them, but they have now become mainstream directly because of their influence. The exotic garden is, in fact, ideal for the busy urban professional because it is low maintenance, very impressive during the growing season and takes advantage of London's mild climate. I love it when I come across a hardy Japanese banana *(Musa basjoo)* growing in front of a house; it's very refreshing to have a taste of something tropical when the skies are grey! The best Japanese banana that I have seen in London was growing in the very small courtyard of an Indian restaurant in Peckham called Ganapati (perhaps they still get the monsoon there?). Of course Kew Gardens, being the show-off it is, has various types of bananas in its tropical glasshouse reaching high into the sky, laden with fruit. But that is inside, so it's to be expected.

The best exotic garden that I've seen in all of Britain was that of Will Giles on a sheltered hill overlooking the suburbs of Norwich. He must have used a hell of a lot of manure and fertilizer because he created a real life jungle in Norfolk with some plants at least 10 foot tall and some maybe even 20! An incredible feat as many of those plants have to reach this size during each growing season.

The best care for exotic plants is to use a fertilizer rich in nitrogen (such as chicken manure in moderation or well-rotted horse manure in quantity), to water frequently as though it's monsoon season and to protect tender growth with fleece in the winter. And that's pretty much it! I remember one writer saying that it was a bit like cottage gardening because you just jumble the plants up and their fantastic form does the talking, as the flowers do in a cottage garden.

Plants that I would recommend are the false castor oil plant (*Fatsia japonica*), either the Abyssinian (*Ensete ventricosum*) or Japanese banana (*Musa basjoo*); bamboos which are not too invasive; *Tetrapanax papyrifer*; *Phormium tenax*; *Cordyline australis*; and *Schefflera rhododendrofolia*. But there are plenty of others that can be used, such as cannas and dahlias, *Verbena bonariensis*, begonias or bedded out houseplants such as the spider plant (*Chlorophytum comosum*).

Going off on a slight tangent, another plant that could be used in exotic gardens, but which is not hardy in Britain, is the real castor oil plant (*Ricinus communis*). It can only be used as bedding during the summer but is none the worse for that as it grows so quickly. Its seeds are deadly poisonous because they contain Ricin, the substance used in the assassination of the Bulgarian defector Georgi Markov in 1978. In that case, the KGB (it is assumed) used a bespoke umbrella that fired a ricin-laced bullet into his leg on Waterloo bridge, which slowly killed him. So always be wary of gardener who has an exotic garden!

*The view from the big window at the back of
The Clocktower onto its 'Sissinghurst style' orchard.*

Sissinghurst

*T*he three English gardens in the South East that garden designers talk about the most are Sissinghurst, Rousham and Great Dixter. All three are very special in their own way but Sissinghurst will always be my favourite despite being tamed by the National Trust's formulaic method of gardening. This is because, in our own amateurish way, my family copied the format of the orchard in our own field with its dovecote, daffodils, long grass and fruit trees. I always think fondly of my father when the daffodils are flowering in March in our field. There is something special about the arrival of the daffodil in early spring — in the strong light of summer they would look decidedly garish but in spring they come as a welcome relief from the dull days of winter.

Nunhead Cemetery

*L*ondon is well-known as a city of green spaces and I feel proud of the horticultural prowess of the Royal Parks in particular. The amount they spend on bedding is more than justified by the tourism it encourages. But there is something more natural about some of the green spaces further out, which are a bit wilder. My personal favourite is Nunhead Cemetery, one of the Magnificent Seven cemeteries, built to deal with the population explosion of the Victorian era. It is now a nature reserve overgrown with sycamores, wild flowers and ivy dotted with tombstones of the most ornate nature (with deliberate Victorian symbolism). My favourite spot is where you come to a small clearing between the trees where an angelic girl stares skyward, ivy twisting round the base of the statue, crumbling the mortar. Frothy cow parsley lights up the clearing and birds sing sweetly. It is perhaps the perfect reminder that without human intervention all our 'Great Cities' would disappear amongst vegetation, leaving us all forgotten however much we lived and loved...

EPILOGUE

Back to the Future with the Cottage Gardener

*I*t's been 10 years since I began The Cottage Gardener in 2008. There have been moments, which I have chronicled earlier in this book, that I have truly hated being a professional gardener. But I think there are always going to be challenges whatever job you do.

In fact, gardening has completely changed my life for the better. In 2003, after dropping out of Edinburgh University, I seemed to have a completely meaningless and sad existence full of anxiety and frustration. Obviously, I still have moments of doubt and self-loathing, but in any finite existence there can be no real happy ending with me walking into the sunset. But things are a lot better than they could have been and every day I thank God, Ganesh or the FTSE (call it what you will) that I was given a second chance. There are many people suffering from acute mental illness that never get that chance. So good-bye for now and here's to savouring every new chapter of the bittersweet symphony that is life.

Goodnight, Hunstanton!

ACKNOWLEDGMENTS

My thanks to Oliver and Lif Marriott whose early advice was invaluable in making this book evolve. But most of all to Mary-Lucille Hindmarch who gave me the tools to turn a rough draft into a book.

I would also like to thank Katie Isbester and her team at Clapham Publishing Services for their support, guidance and patience in producing the book.

She can be reached at:
www.claphampublishing.com

or via email:
contact@claphampublishing.com

Images used on the front and back covers from Botanical illustrations/Visual materials from the papers of John D. Whiting
Artist: Whiting, Grace Spafford
Images from the Library of Congress image archive

Cover and page layout design
Petya Tsankova

Sam MacDonald is a gardener in London, particularly Clapham, where his business, The Cottage Gardener, began in 2008. He specializes in soft landscaping, garden consultancy and bringing gardens to maturity by trying to create a living tapestry of colour between April and October. If you want to contact him or get a copy of the book he can be reached at:

sammacdonald3@hotmail.com

"This book is available from Sam MacDonald at:

sammacdonald3@hotmail.com

It can also be ordered through any bookstore or through Amazon or other eplatforms.